the

Haunted

Volume II

The Wilderness

$\mathcal{L}$. Sydney Fisher

Subscribe to *The Haunted News*
@http://www.LSydneyFisher.com

And remember,
SLEEP WITH THE LIGHTS ON!

Legacy Books Unlimited, Inc.

Books by L. Sydney Fisher

STANDALONES
See No Evil
The Devil's Board

The Phoenix Series
The Phoenix Mission, Part I
The Phoenix Codes, Part II

The Bradford Series
The Haunting of Natalie Bradford, Part I
The Haunting of Natalie Bradford, Part II:
Waking the Dead
The Haunted Prophecy of Natalie Bradford: The
Complete Bradford Series

The Haunted
The Haunted: A Haunted History Series,
Volume I
The Haunted: A Haunted History Series,
Volume II

Author's Note

The Haunted is a collection of true ghost stories in a haunted history series. The settings and characters in the stories are authentic and have been researched and compiled here for your reading pleasure. While the author has taken great measure to ensure accuracy, some scenes may have been dramatized for the sake of storytelling.

Edited by: Independent Literary Services

Cover Design: L. Sydney Fisher

ISBN-13: 978-1976049323
ISBN-10: 1976049326

Dedicated to...

Ghost Lovers
Everywhere

We Believe.

Acknowledgements

Dear Readers,

I must tell you that the absolute best part of researching these books, the history, and the ghost stories is meeting the people who have something special to share. Many of the interviews that I conduct turn into long term friendships, and each and every one of those individuals becomes someone memorable to me. Someone I could never forget as we share our mutual fascination of the afterlife and the question of its existence.

This volume is dedicated to YOU. The believers. The Ghost Lovers everywhere. And to those of you who contributed to these stories, I send you my most sincere thanks.

Susan Bramlett Reid ~ Never doubts me, but always encourages me!
Jamie McMillen ~ My favorite historian whom I admire.
Lisa H. Williams ~ Thank you for sharing your experiences with me. Your story is unforgettable and deserves its own book. You are brave and strong. God Bless.
Martha Jo Coleman ~ My favorite lunch pal and a blessing.
Larry & Hannah Boatwright ~ My favorite conversationalists and kindred souls.
Debbie Bell Summerford ~ Thank you for being a ghost lover!
Kevin Knight ~ Your story is one of the best!
Belinda Haynes McKinion ~ You will always be my favorite Indianette!
Wayne Haynes ~ Thank you for sharing so much history and for making the research fun!
Kim Roberts ~ Thank you for showing me a real haunted house!
Kristin Steele Abbott ~ I loved your story!
Lori Senter Byrd ~ My lifelong, ghost loving friend who makes every moment an adventure!
Kimber Kendrick ~ You are my greatest fan. A cherished friend. And a muse who just won't let me quit writing. Thank you!

"The more enlightened our houses are, the more their walls ooze ghosts." ~ Italo Calvino

Welcome to The Wilderness

Now known as The Land of Hanging Grapes, Pontotoc, Mississippi was once the capitol of the great Chickasaw Nation. The region was nicknamed *The Wilderness* by early settlers eager to stake a claim in the land that covered thousands of acres and was once home to Indigenous people. The vast landscape of hills and valleys, rich and fertile plains, and forest filled with wild game such as bear and cougar was comprised of two Mississippi counties known today as Itawamba (pronounced Ita-wam-ba) and Pontotoc (pronounced Pon-to-toc). But on December 9, 1540, hundreds of years before the first settler stepped foot in the area, Spanish explorer, Hernando De Soto descended upon a Chickasaw village located in South Pontotoc County. He stood atop a ridge overlooking an Indian community of huts with thatched roofs and smaller storage huts filled with corn. The explorer scanned a landscape filled with many fires and gazed upon the hills as he watched clouds of smoke drift up into a snowy sky. In just two weeks, the Spanish explorer and his expedition would be settled into the area where he would spend the remainder of the winter.

By March of 1541, De Soto announced that he would be leaving the area. The announcement was welcome news to the Chickasaws whose kindness and hospitality had begun to wane as De Soto and his men took advantage of the friendly tribe. The men of the Spanish expedition had helped themselves to anything they wanted from the Chickasaws and now demanded two hundred natives to continue on the journey as burden bearers for the expedition.

Two days later, the Chickasaws organized a surprise attack on De Soto's camp setting fires to the huts and killing many of the soldiers. As the battle raged, Francisca Hemetrosa, the only white woman on the expedition and the first European woman to first step foot on American soil, ran back into the burning hut to retrieve a pair of pearls that De Soto had entrusted her with. But as she turned to exit, she became trapped in the doorway and perished in the flames. Legend has it that she was buried among the ruins of the South Pontotoc campsite. Her remains have never been found. Could her spirit still be among the hundreds of ghosts said to still haunt the historic county today?

During the years of 1861-1865, Pontotoc had quite a different history. Census records recorded huge population growth in the 1840's, and Mississippi had been declared the 5th richest state in the Union by 1860. But by 1870, almost all of the county's people were gone. Many lost their lives during the War Between the States while others left the area struggling to survive the aftermath of the war and an annihilated landscape that once fed a thriving community. The Yankees burned much of Pontotoc including Mary Washington College north of the present day town. Citizens reported a bleak scene after being forced to leave their homes and women and children were seen wandering around the downtown area lost and displaced. The once bustling town had become desolate, but the persevering spirit of those left behind brought promise to the town as reconstruction commenced.

From the likes of frontier legend, Davy Crockett or African American opera singer Ruby Elzy (1930's) to Gladys Presley, mother of Rock-n-Roll's legendary King, Elvis Presley, the Mississippi hills of *The Wilderness* have stories of grandeur to tell. It's a place of new beginnings and heartbreaking endings. A place where battles and bloodshed have weaved a history destined to be retold. And beneath the graves of many left behind lies the bodies of unrestful spirits who still roam the streets, trapped by the memories of another time. A time in 1836 when *The Wilderness* was given a new name.

Lochinvar

Perhaps one of the most prominent and haunted antebellum sites in Mississippi is the stately mansion that still stands after the passing of almost two centuries and one tornado in 2001. The home was built around 1842 by Robert Gordon, a Scotsman who migrated to America and formed the towns of Aberdeen and Cotton Gin Port before moving to Pontotoc. Gordon spared no expense on the project after purchasing the land from a Chickasaw woman named Molly Gunn, daughter of William Colbert who was Chief Itawamba's half-brother.

Gordon began construction on the Lochinvar house, named after the site of his Scottish roots, and he employed the skills of Scottish architects and builders. The home's woodwork consisted of heart pine from the area and handmade bricks. Solid Doric style columns delivered to the USA from a castle in Scotland framed the front porch, and the balcony railing was carved in exquisite detail to resemble English lace. Upon entering the front door, guests were awed by the self-supporting spiral staircase that winded to the second floor while a secret staircase in the rear of the home provided a means for servants to enter and exit.

Having established himself as a distinguished proprietor and wealthy statesman, Gordon dreamed of the home's future in Pontotoc as a place of hospitality. The house would be a monument of magnificence honoring his legacy to the area as well as providing an impressive venue for parties. Year after year, the Gordons entertained wealthy friends and travelers at the antebellum home, but after the Civil War outbreak, the mansion narrowly escaped a fiery demise on more than one occasion as Union troops moved through the area.

In 1867, twenty-five years after Lochinvar was built, Robert Gordon died leaving the property to his son, James Gordon. James Jr. loved the family home and the many boyhood memories that it held, especially the memories of learning to fish and hunt with his father by his side. But the one memory that held much significance to Robert Gordon's son was his first true love for a Chickasaw princess named Minti-Ohoyo, Chief Itawamba's daughter. James Jr. expressed his admiration of the Chickasaw maiden in a poem that honors his memory.

Minti-Ohoyo

Minti-Ohoyo was the name of a maiden in the Chickasaw Nation,
The sweetest wild rose on the plain; with lips as red as Carnation.
In English "she comes to me" (Minti-Ohoyo) in Chickasaw tongue.
You bet, I was once sweet upon her – quite "spoony" – but then I was young.
Besides, she was a chief's daughter, Old Itawamba, her sire,
Was the biggest chief in the Nation, but rather addicted to fire.
Firewater, I mean, that the pale-faces gave to the red,
Then cheated them out of their land for which their forefathers bled.

But Mini-Ohoyo, the beauty- Minti-Ohoyo, love's morning star,

Beamed on my heart in my boyhood, my boyhood at old Lochinvar,

"Isito Kobafo" (broken pumpkin) was the Indian name for the place,

Which my father changed into "Lochinvar", the ancient home of his race.

His race that dwelt on the Solway, where the young Laird "came out of the west",

To Netherby Hall, on his swift steed, and bore off the bride to his nest,

With such an ancestor to boast of, no wonder the old Scotchman frowned,

When he saw his heir sweet on an Injun; so he bought up the old chieftain's ground.

And sent Itawamba to westward, the chief and little brown maid,

And I fickle, false lover- forgot every promise I made;

But oft, when weary and careworn, and my heart with its burden o'er teems,

Minti-Ohoyo, the love of my boyhood, comes to me in my dreams."

James Gordon, Jr. lived at and managed his inheritance at Lochinvar until 1893 when he fell into financial disaster. The South's ruin after the Civil War had finally left him homeless. The once wealthy and renowned senator packed his last belongings and with only $4.50 in his pocket, he left Pontotoc for Okolona, Mississippi.

After selling his dog given to him by a friend in Wisconsin, the senator was able to pay the rent on a small homestead where he would eventually establish himself as a dairy farmer. Times had changed, but with hard work and perseverance, the senator was able to establish a lucrative dairy business for his family.

Before his passing on Thanksgiving Day, November 28, 1912, the former senator returned to political office again as he was designated by Mississippi Governor Noel to serve out Senator A. J. McLaurin's last sixty days after McLaurin died.

After his death, James Gordon, Jr. would be fondly remembered as his nickname implied "Sunny Jim", and the memories of his life at Lochinvar would live on through the restless spirits of souls who once protected the cherished grounds.

———⋄———

Stories of a haunted Lochinvar have circulated for more than a century. The home was abandoned for some time after James Gordon, Jr. moved to Okolona, but was later bought by a member of the Fontaine family of Pontotoc before its last sale to Dr. Forrest Tutor and his wife, Dr. Janis Burns-Tutor. Dr. Forrest Tutor has lived in the house since 1968, carefully looking after the place with the same love for Old Lochinvar as James Gordon, Jr. once felt.

The Pontotoc community has a rich history of ghost stories that have come out of the former Lochinvar Plantation. The most noteworthy ghost is believed to be an African American man by the name of Ebenezer who once lived at Lochinvar and served as the plantation's caretaker following the onset of the Civil War. When the War broke out, James Gordon, Jr. organized a cavalry and prepared to leave the home, but before he left he made Ebenezer promise to take care of Lochinvar and not let anyone or anything destroy it. Gordon was fond of Ebenezer and considered him a good friend. He entrusted the mansion and the family he left behind to his friend's watchful eye.

"Uncle Eb", as he was fondly named immediately began his duties as caretaker of the estate. He looked after the family and often entertained James Jr.'s daughter, Annie with stories and outdoor fun on the tree swing. Every evening before nightfall, Uncle Eb made his rounds making sure all doors were locked and the gates were closed. He carried a small gas lantern in his hand as he walked the mansion grounds. Sometimes Uncle Eb was known to wander about the place during the night checking on things and making certain that nothing bad happened on his watch.

One stormy night, Uncle Eb was awakened by an unfamiliar noise. He immediately got out of bed, grabbed his lantern, and roamed the outside grounds searching for the source that had disturbed his slumber. Unable to find anything, Uncle Eb returned to the house, but his clothes were soaked from the rain. Days later, Uncle Eb became ill and began to suffer from symptoms of the common cold, but his condition worsened. In less than one week's time, Uncle Eb had developed pneumonia and died.

Today, people from all over the community have reported seeing the gas lantern's light at Lochinvar after nightfall. Many people believe that Uncle Eb is still looking after the place 150 years later. Other ghostly reports indicate what sounds like conversations between men, but no one is ever found. The sound of horses galloping through the area is also often heard. And there have been numerous reports of stranded motorists at the top of Lochinvar Loop where the entrance to the mansion is situated beneath the trees. Motorists have reported their vehicles stalling at this very spot. There has even been a report of a school bus that traveled the route and experienced the same strange phenomenon every day in the exact same location.

One of the most fascinating accounts of paranormal activity at Lochinvar was reported by a couple of Civil War reenactors who were camped on the Lochinvar grounds. After finishing dinner one evening, the men surveyed the camp and made sure everything was in order before retiring to bed. A few moments later, the men were alerted by the sound of a cavalry regiment moving through the area. The men distinctly heard the undisputable clinking sounds of metal cups and canteens, the crunching sounds of leather saddles as it rubbed against a rider's legs, and the undisputable sound of a horse's trot as it passed by. The men also reported the familiar smell of unwashed horses and humans, and the men said they even felt the vibration of the horses' hooves as the mounted cavalry moved through the camp. The reenactors wasted no time and searched all around while carrying flashlights to illuminate the pitch black wooded area, but nothing was found.

Local ghost enthusiasts consider Lochinvar a classic haunted location. The paranormal activity represents a residual haunting where the energy of a time past still lingers, crossing the veil into the present. The once famous home of a Pontotoc aristocrat now stands steeped in the history of a beloved caretaker and an owner who fought to hold on to his inheritance years after the devastating ruins of the Civil War. Still today, the spirit of Lochinvar's rich and vibrant past can be witnessed among the ghosts of its beloved.

Pontotoc Hospital
Former site of
The Chickasaw Female College

For one hundred years, the site where The Pontotoc Hospital currently stands was home to The Chickasaw Female College, also known as The Pontotoc Female Academy that was founded in 1836. During the early years of settlement, people came to the Pontotoc area from Virginia, Kentucky, and the Carolinas. In addition to their wealth and the servants that they brought with them, they brought teachers to educate their children.

In the spring of 1836, the Presbyterian Conference initiated a prayer for a Christian educational institution for girls, and by November 4, 1836, Thomas C. McMackin, a man renowned to be Pontotoc's founder, donated the land for the project. The school's history began in a one-story, whitewashed building with four windows on the front and back of the building and two chimneys. It was known as one of Pontotoc's finest structures. The institute quickly gained notoriety where a number of subjects were taught such as reading, mathematics, geography, English, history, science, philosophy, astronomy, religion, language, art, and music.

By 1852, the Presbyterians took ownership of the female academy and relocated the institution to the present day site of the Pontotoc hospital. The building was erected of heartwood pine with the walls being three feet thick. Solid brick was used between the rooms making the structure fireproof, and another part of the building's materials consisted of 225,000 bricks that were burned on the college grounds. The college's three story building consisted of an observatory, a chapel on the second floor, and thirty two rooms. A wide veranda stretched across the front of the structure, and the third floor of the building was used as a dormitory for girls.

When the construction had ended and the building was complete, the college was noted as one of the finest structures in Northern Mississippi with its majestic wide portico and grand white columns.

During the institute's early years and before the 1860's, the college was home to many festivities and joyous occasions that included Valentine teas, May Day festivities, dances, and graduations. The town of Pontotoc often hosted hunting parties and barbeques, Fourth of July picnics, and grand balls. This was a time of tranquility. Guests traveled from near and far to attend the town's events, and The Chickasaw Female College was known as a prestigious place to acquire an education.

On April 12, 1861, the War Between the States erupted and the South began its spiraling decline from a land known for its vast wealth to a land of destruction and despair. By the 1860's, The Chickasaw Female College had closed and was being used as a Civil War hospital that housed both Confederates and Union soldiers after The Battle of Corinth and The Battle of Shiloh. Wounded and dying men lined the halls and filled the rooms of the building that once housed the vibrant dreams of young women.

The walls of the institute's beautiful interior became imbedded with the anguish of dying soldiers. The wood floors soaked up the splatters and droplets of a soldier's blood as he screamed in great pain while amputations were performed to save lives. Metal trays were full of bullets that had been removed from the bodies of shot up soldiers struggling to hold on to life while the outside grounds of the college were covered by Confederates who roamed the area, rifles in hand, guarding the three story building from a certain inferno if the Yankees moved in. For four years the Civil War raged on and the schools of Pontotoc were nearly vanished from existence.

Today, The Chickasaw College is a memory of a time when Pontotoc was a thriving community of prestigious citizens and ample progress. Ghostly sightings are not uncommon at the site of the former college. The former site is believed to have at least one intelligent haunting and several residual hauntings that now occupy the area.

Personal accounts of paranormal activity have included being touched by an unseen hand, clothes being pulled by an unseen entity, cold spots, voices heard from unseen sources, and moving shadows throughout the facility. The most chilling encounter continues to dominate the hospital's emergency area and radiology department where the apparition of a female nurse has been seen entering the lab. After an inspection by hospital staff, the lab door was found to be locked from the outside and upon entering the room, the phantom nurse could not be found. Is the nurse the source of the voice being heard or the unseen touches that people repeatedly experience at this location? Was she a nurse who once worked at the hospital and is now eternally connected to the halls that she once walked? Although research did not uncover a possible identity of the ghost, the female nurse spirit is said to be wearing a nurse's uniform relevant to the late 1960's and 1970's era. She is also said to be wearing a nurse's cap.

Strange smells have also been noted by hospital staff. One worker claims to have experienced the odd phenomenon on more than one occasion and has said that the smell is reminiscent of a morgue. Since the hospital does not operate a morgue, the mysterious odor has never been identified but continues to linger near the emergency entrance.

On the outside of the hospital's grounds and near the lake that sits on the lot at the foot of a hill, is an area that is reportedly the home of a Civil War soldier's ghost who roams the landscape beyond the brush and treeline. He has been seen exiting the trees on the left side of the property and has been seen walking across the landscape toward an area of brush a few feet away. He appears as a Confederate infantryman with corporal stripes and wearing a butternut shell jacket, civilian pattern trousers, and black slouch hat with black leather gear. He also is said to be carrying a federal blue covered canteen but does not have a rifle. The ghostly man appears in three dimensional forms for a few seconds before disappearing. Witnesses of this paranormal encounter claim that the Confederate spirit looks completely normal as a living man until he reaches a section of brush on the property where he vanishes. This area has not been investigated to determine whether or not the ghost soldier is capable of communication, but it is believed that the sighting may be more than a residual haunting. The Chickasaw Female College existed for more than one hundred years leaving us with memories of grand times, joyous occasions, and also the bittersweet memories of those who survived their injuries of the War Between the States. For the men who suffered and died here, their spirit remains an eternal imprint.

Pontotoc Courthouse

At the center of downtown Pontotoc, Mississippi stands a three story courthouse complete with a balcony that overlooks the entire city. The first courthouse was built in 1840 and housed the United States court for many years. Prior to the 20th century, the present site of Pontotoc's courthouse was home to a tavern and a hotel owned by Thomas McMackin, the founder of Pontotoc.

During the 1890's, a handsome and famous duelist and United States Marshal named Alexander Keith

McClung frequently stayed here while passing through town. He was often carrying a high profile criminal and a black servant named Caesar who was responsible for guarding these high profile criminals. Caesar was a tall, big man and often times, it was Caesar who roughed up a rowdy prisoner if needed. It has been said that Mr. McClung spent a restless life, rarely sleeping and pacing the floor back and forth all through the night. He didn't sleep well because he was constantly worried that someone was going to kill him. When exhaustion finally took over, he would collapse into a chair or sofa with his gun in his hand as he snoozed.

The Pontotoc Courthouse is also the site where Vernon Presley and Gladys Smith applied for a marriage license on June 17, 1933. Their famous son, Elvis Aaron Presley was later born in Tupelo, Mississippi on January 8, 1935.

The present day courthouse in Pontotoc was established in 1915 and celebrated its opening months later in December, 1916. The building's classic design was constructed of white stone that towered three stories high with a basement that was used for county offices. The courtroom, jury and witness room, and judge's office were all located on the second floor. The third floor was designed to be used as a dormitory for jurors during lengthy trials. During the Civil War, the original courthouse, situated in the middle of Confederate Park, was spared from a fiery demise by the Union because two of the building's wings were constructed by the Federal Government.

Stories of paranormal activity at this location have been experienced by a number of people over the course of several decades. Reports consist of feeling as if they are being watched, strange noises such as footsteps when no one is there, loud crashes, and at least one sighting of a male apparition dressed in a brown broad rim hat (fedora style), dark colored button down shirt, and brown boots who was seen walking toward the west end door of the courthouse before disappearing. And the ghost of a woman carrying a baby has been spotted near the outside front steps of the courthouse.

Another disturbing incident involved an interaction with an unseen force on the building's uppermost floor. One day while viewing old court records that were stored on the third floor, someone claimed that an unseen presence stalked every move they made while they examined the records. Strange tapping noises and scraping sounds echoed throughout the halls while footsteps were heard just inches away from them. They reported a feeling of someone hovering over them, watching. The person who asked to remain anonymous stated that within a few minutes the atmosphere had almost become unbearable. After experiencing an overwhelming sense of anger and dread, they rushed out of the room and down the stairs to the first floor exit. This type of paranormal activity at the Pontotoc Courthouse earns this site the right to claim a possible intelligent haunting by an angry ghost who stalks its victims until they leave. Could the ghost be a former prisoner who received an ill-fated sentence long ago?

Post Office Museum

By 1900, there were 26 post offices in Pontotoc County. Distributing mail was much more difficult compared to today's methods. Mail carriers used horse drawn carriages or wagons, and the postman often carried hot bricks along to warm their feet during cold weather. A few years later, most of Pontotoc county's 26 post offices had been phased out. The last of these post offices to close its door was Springville. It was once named the smallest post office (10x12) in the United States by

Ripley's Believe It or Not. It closed for good in December, 1956 after 80 years of operation.

The present post office museum is now home to a variety of historical exhibits. The famous painting of De Soto's visit to Pontotoc hangs just inside the door. It was painted by Joseph Polletin in 1939 and depicts the first Christian marriage on the North American continent between Juan Ortiz and Saowana, a Seminole princess. The marriage ceremony took place in Pontotoc on Christmas Day, 1540.

This post office is believed to house the ghost of a former postmaster or caretaker. During a visit by a professional paranormal investigator some years ago, the ghost made himself known in a room on the lower floor. According to the investigator's report, the ghost was standing near the tower ladder which he frequently climbed to stand watch over the building. The entity is described as a Caucasian male standing approximately 5'10" tall with dark brown hair and a beard matching the same. He is said to be wearing dark colored trousers and has been seen sitting in a chair inside an undisclosed room that is used for exhibits in the museum.

Another psychic medium visited the museum in 2012. The medium reported more than one haunting at the museum's location. In addition to the intelligent haunting of a male ghost, there appears to be residual energy in the main exhibit hall where the medium identified the location as a former site of execution by fire. Later research confirmed that the Chickasaws had burned people at the stake in what is now downtown Pontotoc and before settlers moved in.

Today, Pontotoc's Post Office Museum is the only historical working post office in the United States. Visitors here can retrace the steps of the Chickasaw Nation and learn about the early pioneers who settled here. And if you get really lucky, the museum's immortal exhibit just might show up in the secret room on the bottom floor.

The Lady Congress

Named after Main Street which was originally called Congress Street, this two story brick home is located in downtown Pontotoc and was built in 1854 by a man named Thielgeld. The house is one of Pontotoc's oldest surviving structures with a fascinating history that precedes itself. Mr. Thielgeld lived in the home for a few years and boarded a room out to Fannie Ratliff Brown and her husband, Professor Brown who was the principal of the Pontotoc Male Academy.

One day Professor Brown severely whipped a student by the name of Carey Wray. The boy went home at the noon recess and showed the whip marks to his family. The boy's older brother, Keith Wray became enraged. He grabbed a nearby knife that was used for cutting paper and bolted out the door intent on getting revenge against Professor Brown.

As Professor Brown was walking home, Keith Wray confronted him on the sidewalk located directly across from the present day location of the house. The two of them exchanged a few hostilities before Keith stabbed the professor in the heart several times killing him. The professor's lifeless body fell to the ground in a pool of blood. His wife, Fannie and Mr. Thielgeld's daughter watched the professor from Fannie's bedroom window on the second floor.

Mrs. Fannie fainted and fell to the floor upon seeing her husband murdered right before her eyes. Then tragedy struck again the following day when Mr. Thielgeld's daughter died of Typhoid Fever. Keith Wray was held in the Holly Springs jail for two years before he was acquitted after the Governor of Virginia sent $1,000 for his legal fees. Wray's father was a personal friend of Governor Wise because he had saved the governor's life in a duel some years before.

Not long after this, Dr. William Slack, president of Mary Washington College came to live here. He remained here for thirty-two years, and it is this time that holds some of the house's most intriguing history. Dr. Slack witnessed the Civil War's effect on Pontotoc from this home and watched as the town struggled to survive during the Reconstruction Era. Dr. Slack was also a physician and minister of Pontotoc's First Baptist Church. Church congregations often gathered here to be baptized in Molly Walker Pond located behind the house. Dr. Slack was well-known in the community for his compassion and servitude.

During the Civil War, Dr. Slack opened the doors of this home to any person or family needing medical attention. Amputations were performed here and the arm and bones of some have been unearthed on the property. Surgical saws, medical instruments, and other artifacts such as old medicine bottles have also been uncovered here.

Years later in 1934, Dr. J.A. Rayburn and his son, Dr. T.H. Rayburn bought the house and opened Pontotoc's first official hospital here. There were eight beds available for patients, and visitors were received in what is now a large living room on the first floor. The x-ray and laboratory equipment were also located on the ground floor.

The hospital carried a significant distinction as the birthplace of United States Senator, Thad Cochran, musician Delaney Bramlett, and Kermit Scott, whose best friend, Jim Henson, named his most famous muppet character, Kermit the Frog after him. This house also served as a hospital and was used to house patients from the Tupelo tornado of 1936 that leveled forty-eight city blocks.

Another notable death that occurred here when the house was used as The Pontotoc Clinic was the death of local psychologist and clairvoyant, Seymour Prater. Mr.

Prater was a patient at the clinic for several weeks in 1945. He entered the clinic in February and died from a brain tumor on a Saturday and at the exact hour of his birth 78 years before, April 21, 1867. His date of death is listed as April 21, 1945. Seymour Prater was known throughout the Southeast for his uncanny abilities to find lost objects and solve mysteries using what he called his "radio mind". In August 2016, L. Sydney Fisher published a book titled, *See No Evil* that was inspired by a real life murder that happened in Carroll County, Mississippi on January 3, 1931 when Arthur Floyd was brutally attacked in his store and left saturated in blood near the front entrance to the store. Without Seymour Prater's assistance, the Floyd family might never have known any closure in the senseless death of their brother and loved one.

This property is now used as a private residence where a number of discarnate spirits still call it home. Residual hauntings exist throughout this property earning The Lady Congress bragging rights as one of the most haunted locations in Pontotoc. Unfamiliar smells, moving objects, dancing lights, and voices are just some of the paranormal activity attached here.

At one time, the house was also used as a boarding school. Two teachers who were sisters once lived here. Neither of them ever married and could often be heard arguing with each other. Today, those conversations can still be witnessed from time to time as the two women carry on with their discussions in a bedroom once occupied by the spinsters.

Other ghostly sightings have included a full body apparition descending from the second floor and down the staircase. The man was described as wearing an officer's Confederate uniform with a hat, but he appeared to be transparent. He walked to the third step from the floor and then disappeared.

Another ghostly encounter included a full three dimensional sighting. One morning when a guest had been staying overnight in the home and sleeping on the sofa in the downstairs den, he was awakened by someone speaking to him. He opened his eyes and saw an African

American man standing over him. The unknown man stared down at the guest and repeatedly said to him, "I am sorry. I am so sorry." Then without warning, the man who had appeared to be a living being suddenly vanished. The guest jumped off the sofa and left. He refused to spend another night in the house from that day forward.

The owners of the home today say that the energy there is peaceful and happy. Although they have experienced phenomena that cannot be explained by logical means, they say that they feel a sense of kinship to the spirits who still reside at one of Pontotoc's most cherished homes, The Lady Congress.

The Colbert Place

One of the most significant and famous sites of the Chickasaw Nation rests among Magnolia and Cedar trees with its foundation situated several feet from what is now Highway 6 West. The house at the Bissell Community in Tupelo, Mississippi is said to be the oldest surviving home in Lee County, Mississippi. Two centuries ago, the area was still known as Pontotoc County, and the house was owned by Chief Tishomingo, also known as James Colbert, one of four

Colbert brothers who greatly influenced the Chickasaw tribe.

History tells us that the oldest brother, William Colbert once visited President George Washington who gave the Chickasaw chief a shovel dedicated in the president's name as a symbol of growth and prosperity if the Chickasaws would adopt the ways of the settlers and cultivate the land for raising crops, cattle, and swine. Colbert returned home with the shovel which he displayed in his home, often bragging to guests about the shovel's significance.

Another visit to the president's residence in Philadelphia proved to have a lasting impact on The Colbert Place. According to the story, members of the Chickasaw Delegation were invited by Washington to stop by his home at Mt. Vernon. Before departing, Washington offered the Chickasaw Interpreter, Malcolm McGee, a sprig of a Weeping Willow tree from his lawn. McGee returned to Colbert's place and planted the sprig on the farm at Bissell. It is said that the sprig given by President George Washington became the "progenitor" of all the Weeping Willows in Lee County, Mississippi.

The Colbert Place was also known as Colbert's Tavern and was a designated stagecoach stopping point along the Old Natchez Trace. Colbert's mother, Saleechie, became famed for her delicious cooking of wild game. Legend has it that here under an ancient oak tree, the last king of the Chickasaw Nation was elected one day in the month of June, 1820. King's Creek that runs through the city of Tupelo was named after King Ishtohotopah.

Decades later, The Colbert Place's history and its ghostly legends are still talked about. Some have claimed that the area still harbors the residual energy of those who once passed here.

James Colbert, Chief Tishomingo died in Arkansas during the journey west with his people. He was 100 years old.

The Pontotoc Cemetery

For decades, ghost stories have circulated about this historic cemetery in Pontotoc, Mississippi. The burial site had its beginnings with the graves of Civil War soldiers, and later with the grave of Ruby Elzy, an African American opera singer who appeared on stage, radio, and film.

Donated by the Chickasaw Indians and the U.S. Government, its earliest known burial was in 1836. The graves in this cemetery contain soldiers from all wars since 1812 and include one hundred twenty-three Confederate dead.

One of the most notable graves in the cemetery belongs to Major General William Colbert, a Chickasaw chief who served the United States at the Battle of The Fallen Timbers in 1794 and again in the War of 1812. The oldest son of James Logan Colbert, a Scotsman who migrated to Mississippi in the 1700's, died here in 1836 as the Chickasaw people began making their journey to Oklahoma. His body is believed to be among other unmarked Chickasaw graves.

Reports of paranormal phenomena and its occurrence here have circulated for decades. Strange balls of light have been seen dancing above the tombstones during nightfall. And other fascinating tales have included sightings of a three dimensional form sitting on top of the tombstones near Major General Colbert's marked grave. The ghostly form was said to be transparent.

Are the ghosts of former soldiers still lingering in the cemetery where they were buried?

Save - A - Lot

During Pontotoc's early beginnings, the location where this grocery store currently stands was known as the rowdy side of the county. Years ago before the current retail development, cattle barns dotted the landscape here, and it was a popular hangout post for whiskey lovers and rascals looking for trouble.

Stories of a poltergeist here have circulated for years. Strange phantom voices have been heard and objects have mysteriously flown off the shelves of aisles where no one was present. Witnesses claim that a doll once became possessed by some unseen presence.

The story goes that one night when workers were in the store next door to the Save-A-Lot (all the stores are located in one large building), the workers were restocking and organizing the shelves. Two of the workers were having friendly conversation when all of a sudden one of them heard something fall from a shelf and onto the floor. The sound of wicked laughter followed. The two workers then followed the sounds to investigate. When they turned the corner of the aisle, they noticed that a doll was lying face up in the floor as if it had been positioned there, and it was laughing. One of the workers reached down to pick up the doll, but just as her hands touched the doll's mid-section, it stopped.

The worker checked the switch on the doll's box and became overwhelmed by a chilling revelation. The switch was turned to OFF. She threw the doll down hard and fast then rushed out of the area.

Another reported incident involved a shadow figure seen through one of the main windows on this property. The witness claims that upon returning to their car after a quick shopping excursion, they noticed a strange, dark figure hovering in the window of a furniture store. The figure began zipping madly about the center of the store then abruptly stopped and faced the witness who was now staring in disbelief. Then the shadow man began to walk with a fast pace toward the window. The witness then jumped into their vehicle and raced out of the area. Shaking in disbelief and filled with terror, they vowed not to ever return.

Are the Save-A-Lot store and its vicinity somehow linked to a restless spirit who refuses to move on? Could the poltergeist experienced at the store actually be a ghost capable of communicating with the living, or does it just want to frighten unsuspecting people who stumble into its domain? Perhaps the ghost was one of the 'rascals' who once occupied the site but now lives out an eternity as an earthbound spirit seeking wicked fun.

The Legend of the Rosalba Ghost

During the mid-1800's, Colonel Richard Bolton operated a wheat mill on land that occupied his home just outside the current day Pontotoc city limits. The Colonel built the mill and the mill pond in 1850 during a time of prosperity when Mississippi farmers thrived. Bolton purchased the mill's engine from a cotton factory in Georgia and had it transported to Pontotoc. His home was built near the mill and named Rosalba after the exquisite white rose vines that draped the front porch.

Bolton's mill was the only mill within a fifty mile radius. Farmers often camped for days near the mill while waiting to have their wheat grinded into soft, white flour. Also located on the property was a rustic inn that offered camping, boating, and fishing privileges for a nominal fee.

Years later, wheat farming declined in the region, and the mill closed. The lake and surrounding area was transformed in the early twentieth century into a recreational lake and campgrounds for the community. Families and visitors enjoyed the amenities that the grounds offered during its heyday in Pontotoc County, Mississippi.

Rosalba was a name associated with Pontotoc's history and memories of family gatherings at the lake. Historic memories that have now become shadowed by a mystery that has never been solved. Sometime during the 1920's, it is believed that a young woman was murdered near the lake after leaving a dance. Her body was rumored to have been dumped somewhere between the land surrounding the lake and Pontotoc city limits. No one has ever identified the ghostly woman, but many have claimed to have seen her spirit wandering the hills of Rosalba Road searching for her murderer. The area was never known to harbor the souls of the deceased until word of the mourning woman's ghost began to appear.

The ghost is said to mourn for her untimely death on the night that she was lured near the lake by a man she had met at the dance. The young lovers flirted and played until something went deadly wrong, and the young woman found herself struggling against a suitor turned attacker. Her screams were silent as she fought wildly against a certain fate, and her breath shortened as the hands of her beau tightened around her neck. With her last breath, she stared with horror into the eyes of her attacker. Her attacker then hastily dumped her body in the hidden brush of the Pontotoc hills, hiding his guilt and burying the body of a woman whose soul would never rest. It's said that late at night if you're traveling the hills of Rosalba Road, you may just encounter the ghostly legend of Rosalba Lake.

A Haunting at Ecru

This small town in Pontotoc County covers a land mass of approximately 4.1 miles with a population of 969 people according to the 2014 census. But the town's population involves an up and down record of growth and decline since the early twentieth century when records reported a population surge of 35 percent by 1920.

The early settlers of Ecru, Mississippi were mostly Irish with English and German being the lesser percentile of today's descendants. The town was said to be named after the small post office that was first opened here and whose exterior walls were painted an ecru color.

Pontotoc County saw a number of skirmishes during the War Between the States. The area was invaded by the Union who burned Mary Washington College that was located not far from the small town. Soldiers camped and traveled in and out of the area for more than four years while the war lingered, leaving the small town with a ghost story of its own.

Jake Denton Road is a county road in Ecru, Mississippi. Many witnesses agree that the area is haunted by a one hundred and fifty year old unidentified ghost. Numerous reports of a Confederate soldier's transparent apparition have been seen in a field across from the main road. The ghostly figure has also been sighted walking across the field and toward a nearby house where the soldier was said to have walked into the outside wall.

The locals believe that the soldier is protecting the place. Is it possible that this Confederate soldier was killed and buried somewhere in the field? Or could he be a residual haunting otherwise known as a permanent recording of a moment in time when he was, in fact, guarding the nearby railroad?

A Haunting in Algoma

This small town in Pontotoc County gets its name from a word that means "vale of flowers". The community located in South Pontotoc comprises an area of 6.6 square miles with a population of approximately 600 people as of the 2014 census. Although the town is small, its history in the southern region of the county is vast and dates historic records at least two centuries ago.

During the winter of 1540, Hernando De Soto camped south of Algoma in an area now known as

Redland. The lush forests, natural creeks, and rolling hills provided a rich landscape for hunting deer, panther, and bear. During the Civil War, the southern part of the county saw skirmishes between the Yankees and Rebels on more than one occasion and most notably during the days before The Battle of Tupelo at Harrisburg.

This area is also linked to the Old Natchez Trace, a historic trail that is said to be 10,000 years old. The Old Trace extends approximately 440 miles and travels through three states; Mississippi, Alabama, and Tennessee.

Legends of the Trace include tales of buried treasures, ghost stories, outlaws, Indian traders, and witches. And one of the most recent ghost sightings may very well be attached to a weary traveler who once walked the dark and mysterious path.

Ghost sightings are not uncommon to the Trace, but one such haunting seems to be attached to a home located on Algoma Road. The male apparition has shown himself on several occasions, often pausing to stare back at a stunned witness. He has been described as wearing a long jacket, dark trousers, and a weathered hat with a floppy brim that appears to be tattered and worn. The witness says that he has thin lips and appears to stand approximately 6'0" tall. He also has been seen at other locations on the property, and always responds to human encounters in the same manner. With a curiosity that only a ghost could understand. He watches and studies the homeowner, sometimes leaned up against the wall as if he is taking a rest before fading out of sight.

Sometime later, the owner of this home contacted a medium who came out and investigated the area. Upon inspection of the home, the medium identified a portal that the ghost was most likely using to enter the house and instructed the owner to move a mirror that was hanging next to a window.

Using drawings of the ghost that the homeowner created from the encounters, the medium concluded that the spirit was a Civil War soldier still attached to the area and possibly buried nearby.

The homeowner removed the mirror with hopes that the portal, otherwise known as the doorway between the living world and the dead, had been closed. No other paranormal phenomena have been reported.

PART II

FULTON, MISSISSIPPI

Itawamba County

The Ghosts of Haunted Hill

No other location in Fulton, Mississippi has come close to the ghostly thrills experienced on Haunted Hill. Located off the square in downtown Fulton, the house sits off the main street of this small town and is situated on a tranquil, corner lot shaded by a century old Oak tree. The home's Old World and European architectural design has been a head turner for decades. Still today, the home's hillside landscape filled with lush green grass and flowering shrubs creates a beautiful curbside scene as passersby made their way toward the west part of town.

During the early 1920's, a new funeral director moved to town and built his business just a few blocks away from the house that was later constructed from 1938-39. From 1929-1961, the mortician and his family ran the local funeral home, but by 1971, the house sat vacant.

Then in the summer of 1971, Tom and Anita Williams moved into the home with their four children. The house brought new hopes and dreams for the family as it provided ample space for the kids to roam and play while Anita enjoyed the extra downstairs rooms that the family's mobile home had lacked. But there was no way the family could have known that Mr. Cartledge had often used the basement for embalming bodies.

Not long after moving into their dream home, the ghostly activity began to manifest as shadows danced across the rooms, lingering just long enough to catch a glimpse of them. The Williams' youngest child, Emmalee, began seeing the haunting figures by the age of two. The growing toddler even named two of her frequent ghostly visitors, Walket and Staypid, which may have been translated to Walker and David. She often reported seeing apparitions hiding behind the curtains of the home, and the young girl often spoke of the elderly man in the attic bedroom. While it's true that children have vivid imaginations, the later sightings and paranormal phenomena were too frequent and unnerving to be dismissed as a creative manifestation.

Months went on as the ghosts began to appear more frequently. Tom and Anita's only son reported seeing the ghost of a woman standing near his bed every morning. He became awakened by her visits each day as she would shake his bed and move his things about the room.

The couple's oldest daughter also reported seeing a blond haired woman sitting in the rocking chair downstairs. Sometimes the empty chair would rock back and forth.

The ghosts were also known to play the piano, turn the lights off and on, and rearrange the family's personal belongings. But the most disturbing encounter with one of the spirits involved the female entity's interaction with Anita Williams late one evening when Anita was alone in her bedroom watching television.

Anita's oldest daughter was expected home at any time on this particular night. The day had been uneventful on Haunted Hill, and Anita was relaxing in her bedroom at the rear of the house when something caught her attention in the connecting hall. Movement caught Anita's eye. The figure of a woman with blond hair walked steadily toward her room. Thinking it was her daughter returning home, she called out and asked "Is that you?", but no response came, and the ghostly figure continued to walk toward the room. Seconds later, the phantom woman entered Anita's bedroom and turned toward the bathroom. Anita immediately looked up as the woman remained silent. She walked toward the bathroom door and began to turn around to face Anita as Anita stared back with cold chills now covering her body. As the phantom woman turned, Anita saw that the figure staring back at her was not her daughter. The ghost then reached out toward a door that wasn't there and leaned forward as if pulling it shut toward her. As she closed the invisible door, the ghost woman smiled at Anita and faded out of sight.

To this day, the female ghost has not been identified. Local townsfolk have also reported seeing the apparition of a blond haired woman standing in the front window of the house. Family members have speculated that it could have been the spirit of someone who once lived on the property. Years before the mortician built the home, the town boasted some of the finest school academies around. Some people have suggested that the lot may have housed a former girl's boarding school, and the ghost could be a former teacher still attached to the area where she once taught. Emmalee, Anita and Tom's youngest daughter has speculated that her old man ghost could have been the former owner of the home.

Few hauntings have as many witnesses as this house on Haunted Hill. The frequency of ghost sightings and the numerous unexplained phenomena make this historic home's story a haunted treasure with cinematic appeal. Its stories are timeless and will continue to be cherished by ghost lovers of this town for decades to come.

The Devil's Den

There's a place in Itawamba County, Mississippi, deep in the woods of Highway 25 North where spirits manifest from unexplained sources causing terror and unrest for all those who venture here. Although no one knows the exact history of the location, it is believed to be the former home of ancient Indians. Others have speculated that the lot may have been the site of a church or cemetery. But the house and hillside lot is now known to be inhabited by multiple spirits who have been known to communicate with the living.

The house was built in the late 1990's and has known more than one family who has taken up residence here and then left with nothing more than tragic memories of loss and ruin. But the property's haunted past may have begun more recently in 2008 when a woman gave birth to a baby boy in the bathroom and then later confessed to killing the infant and stuffing its body in a bucket that was placed inside a 55-gallon drum.

Relatives discovered the decomposing body days later at the end of the driveway near the home. An autopsy was performed on the five pound infant and revealed that the boy's lungs were functioning after birth. Within three days of the grimly discovery, the mother confessed to the murder and was charged with depraved heart murder.

Months later, the house sat empty and abandoned until an unsuspecting family moved in. The Benton family was excited by the idea of a large, roomy home with a basement and built on a hillside that overlooked acres of trees. Surrounded by the serenity of the forest and its beauty, the family of five settled into the property without any knowledge of its past. They had high hopes of making the house a home where they would be raising their children, but weeks later they found themselves being stalked by something they couldn't explain.

Evil laughter, loud slamming, and banging noises were heard inside the house from time to time, and the full body apparition of a tall woman with hollow, black eyes and gray skin was seen peering through the curtains of the foyer window. The hunchback elderly woman's ghost was seen on the porch where the sound of ghostly children running and playing had also been heard.

The Benton kids also reported seeing a massive black shadow person around the property and inside the house. The black shadow was seen running away from the house toward the woods on several occasions. It was at least seven to eight feet tall and almost equaled in width. The shadow was able to change its shape and lift itself off the ground.

The Benton's family pets may have been the first to notice the unwelcome entities. Within a week of moving in, the family cat refused to enter one of the rooms in the house, and the dog often hid behind the fireplace, refusing to come out. But the most reported activity in the house appeared to be in the basement. One family member reported being shoved down the stairs leading into the basement. Robert Benton suffered carbon monoxide poisoning while working in the underground room, and Leslie Benton reported that something rubbed her hair on two different occasions.

Doorknobs were seen turning and sounds of running water were heard in the master bedroom, but the source of the mysterious sound was never discovered. Perhaps the most terrifying event witnessed during the family's time in the house was the psychological changes that Robert Benton underwent before his death. Changes that can only be explained by the influences of a dark and sinister presence that tormented him for weeks.

Robert Benton was a commercial truck driver and a healthy, hardworking man with a loving wife and family until bizarre mood swings began to consume him. Family members reported hearing him talk to himself, often having conversations with an invisible person. As weeks passed, Robert became more hostile, lashing out at the rest of the family. His outbursts were characterized by heavy cursing and violent threats.

One day Robert was restocking his truck and preparing for a trip when he heard children's voices coming from the sleeper bunk. He climbed into the driver's side of the cab and noticed two elementary aged kids sitting in front of him and having a conversation. He called out to them.

"Hey, what are you kids doing up here? Who are you?"

But the kids seemed oblivious to Robert's presence or were simply ignoring him. Then he called out again.

"Hey, who are you?" Robert stared at them in bewilderment. Then he gasped as one of the children asked the other.

"Is he dead?"

Robert quickly extended his hand, reaching to touch its arm when both of the children suddenly vanished right before his eyes. The eerie encounter had been nothing more than an unexplained experience with the dead. Although Robert was visibly shaken, he kept the bizarre encounter a secret, telling only his uncle about what he had witnessed. Without a doubt, the appearance of the children as two full bodied apparitions may have been a harbinger of tragedy about to strike an innocent family.

Days later on a sunny afternoon, another family relative (uncle) was on the main wrap-a-round porch rummaging through a box that was sitting next to an empty chair and a set of hanging wind chimes. When the man stood up from the box, he jumped back at the sight of a ghostly figure before him. There sitting in the chair was an elderly woman staring straight ahead, her eyes fixed in a catatonic state. The man gasped and grabbed the wind chimes that had now started to swing back and forth. In one hard fast swing, he slung them over the porch railing and ran inside the house.

Two weeks later on an early Saturday morning, Robert Benton awakened and got dressed. He gathered his wife's cell phone and car keys and hid them where she would not be able to find them. He then went downstairs to the basement and cut the phone lines to the inside of the house.

Something else had taken over Robert Benton's personality. Before the day was gone, he stood at the center of the stairs and took his own life. With a shotgun in his hand, he muttered his last words to an unseen entity that had been tormenting him.

Leslie Benton stayed in the house for a short time after her husband's burial. She struggled to make sense of everything that had happened. Nothing could explain the changes that Robert Benton had undergone leading up to the day he died, but she remembered seeing her husband sitting on the porch weeks before his death shaking his head 'no' as if he was talking to someone. He later told her that he was experiencing unsettling thoughts.

Determined to find answers, she turned to TAPS of Alabama, a paranormal investigative team who came out and conducted a full paranormal investigation with cameras and audio recordings. TAPS of Alabama provided recorded documentation of the investigation that included disembodied voices heard in the house's basement. Of the recorded voices, the distinct words 'help me', 'baby', and 'Chris die' were heard. One of the investigators was named Chris.

While the team was investigating the property, they also experienced paranormal phenomena when they left one of their devices (EMF recorder) sitting on a table. While the device was on and picking up unknown magnetic energy fields, it inexplicably fell off the table and slid across the floor.

At the conclusion of the paranormal investigation, TAPS of Alabama advised the family that there was enough evidence to label the property 'haunted'. Leslie Benton then reached out to the local Catholic Church who sent a representative to bless the property.

After the cleansing of the house and property, the activity calmed. But today, the spirits still remain.

A Note from Sydney: I visited this site in June, 2017 while conducting research for this book. When I arrived at the end of a long gravel drive, I met a lady named Alicia who was a friend of the Benton family. She and I talked for a few minutes, and then she showed me around the property. Although the house was empty with all entry doors locked, we were able to peer through the windows and see inside the house.

During the brief time that I was there, I witnessed some of the mysterious noises behind the closed basement door. Shuffling and sliding noises. Thumping and banging. While I was on the porch, I felt as if someone was watching me, and I immediately sensed the presence of an old woman near the front window. The feeling was strong enough that I wanted to leave.

I then walked to my car and talked with Alicia for a few minutes. The feeling of 'wanting to leave' became almost overwhelming. I looked around the property, scanning the area and suddenly saw a strange black shadow racing back and forth in front of the trees. I did not say anything to Alicia about it and just continued to watch it move up and down and back and forth while she told me about the history of the place. I even blinked my eyes a few times thinking that might erase what I was seeing, but as I stood near the end of the driveway, I watched the shadow expand in width and height as it climbed several feet off the ground. At that point, I thanked Alicia and got in my car and left. Fast.

I always approach 'haunted' sites with skepticism. Most of the time, there is a logical explanation for suspected paranormal phenomena, but not this time. The energy at this place took three days for me to shake off. Something is definitely there. And no further investigating is necessary to convince me.

The Ghost of Cummings Street

The cottage style homes that line Cummings Street today in Fulton, Mississippi were once a part of a quaint neighborhood filled with the sounds of children's laughter as they played on the nearby grounds of Fulton Grammar School. Many of the homes were built in the 1940's during a residential construction boom in the area that covered several square miles. The proximity of the school was a welcome amenity for families with children. Kids often walked to school and back home in the afternoon, and the area was considered one of the safest neighborhoods in the city. Today the houses are still a popular buy for small families, retirees, and newlyweds, but one of the most charming cottages on the corner has a history and a ghostly tenant who has made the house his eternal home.

The blue trimmed, three-bedroom home was built in 1942 and sold many years later to a single mother with two children. The family moved into the home in the early 1980's with little knowledge of the home's history except for its previous owners. No one had any reason to suspect that paranormal activity was about to welcome them, but within months of moving in, Sandy Dawson and her teenage daughter began experiencing things they could not explain.

Lights in the house flickered on and off and the breaker box in the laundry room almost caught fire. Even after repairs were done, breakers would still go out in the dead of night making flashlights a necessity to keep nearby.

During the eerie blackouts, Sandy's teenage daughter, Leeann often felt as if she was being watched. One night while she was lying in bed, she felt someone's hand slid across the bottom of the bed. She jerked her feet back and quickly sat up; staring into the dimly lit room, but no one was there.

Months later, the creepy feeling returned but this time when she opened her eyes, she found herself staring into the eyes of a man now standing over her and studying her. Leeann gasped, and the man dressed in a painter's clothes disappeared before her eyes.

Sandy Dawson also reported seeing the male apparition while she was in the master bedroom. According to Leeann, her mother witnessed the ghost walk across the room in front of her. She said that Sandy closed her eyes and began to pray. When she opened her eyes the entity was gone, but her nerves were still rattled days later. The Dawson's never discovered who the mystery ghost was or why he was there, but there was one story that might explain who he was.

Years earlier, there was a water tower used to supply the city's neighborhoods located a short distance behind the home. Routine maintenance was performed on the tower that included painting the exterior of its reservoir. Men hired to do the restoration would climb onto platforms that were anchored to the ground. Secured only by a harness that strapped across their waist and fastened to a safety rope, the painters would work for hours blasting off old chipped paint and brightening its concrete exterior with a fresh coat of color. Unfortunately, the helmets, harness, and safety ropes weren't sufficient to save the life of a painter who fell from the one hundred thirty foot tank to his death.

Could the ghost of Cummings Street be one of the many painters who lost his life there? And if so, why is he still an earthbound spirit?

The Spirit of Sheffield Manor

Hidden from the street's main view and situated at the end of a long, narrow drive is a historic home surrounded by fourteen acres of lush vegetation that includes the sweet smell of the Magnolia tree. The stately farmhouse was built in 1912 by Isaac and Anna Rogers Sheffield. Isaac Lewis Sheffield was a prominent Fulton attorney and married Anna Rogers Walker, the daughter of Dr. James Walker, a Fulton physician. Dr. Walker gifted the newlyweds several acres, and the couple soon constructed a modest farmhouse on the property. The couple raised six children in the home, two boys and four daughters.

Years later, the farmhouse changed owners several times and underwent extensive renovations that included the addition of a workshop building and a barn. Today the home is owned by prominent realtor, Kevin Knight who purchased the home in August, 2015. Soon after, Mr. Knight discovered he had a familial connection to the place. And the story of how he came to be the new owner in a home with a past unknown to him before his purchase was almost as uncanny as the ghost who still lingers here.

Kevin Knight visited the Sheffield place many times during the years leading up to his purchase. Although he had no idea of any connection to the place, he couldn't dismiss the fact that each time he found himself at the home for an event or business related visit, he sensed something special about the place. Something that would later be revealed.

Earlier in 2015, Mr. Knight had bought a cabin retreat on the outskirts of Fulton when he suddenly decided to buy Sheffield Manor. Several weeks later, he found himself moving into the grand home and placing a 'for sale' sign on the rustic cabin he had just settled in not long before. But it was a move that seemed to be driven by an inexplicable force as he soon discovered that Sheffield Manor had once been owned by a family relative. Kevin Knight's great-great grandmother had been Isaac Sheffield's sister. Issac Sheffield, the original owner and builder of the house was Kevin Knight's great-great uncle!

Perhaps that might explain the mysterious apparitions that have been seen in the front second floor windows of the home. And the sound of children running across a hardwood floor has also been heard in the home, a common occurrence where residual energy remains. During the years of Sheffield Manor's decline, neighborhood kids played near the home, often running away at the sound of phantom gunfire that could never be explained. A thorough research of the property later revealed that the fourteen acres where Sheffield Manor currently resides was once the home of Confederate artillery.

The century old home and property has all the makings and charm of a true southern haunting, but the most fascinating paranormal phenomena have been sightings of a ghostly apparition moving through the dining room. Although the room was renovated and walls moved, the room is believed to be Isaac and Anna Sheffield's master bedroom. The ghost has never manifested into a full body apparition but instead appears as a dark, misty form that moves quickly across the room and is often seen from the open doorway that leads into a small living room.

Just inside the living room door is the focal point of the room, an antique fireplace original to the home. Sitting on the far right corner of the mantle is a small family picture, and inside the antique brass frame is the face of Kevin Knight's great-great uncle, Isaac Lewis Sheffield.

Could the transient shadow be the ghost of Isaac Sheffield still walking across his old bedroom floor? Perhaps his spirit still lingers here now, stirred by the welcome presence of his great-great nephew.

The Bedford Haunting

For decades, the Bedford family kept secrets about the strange things that happened in the little house by the river. The home was steeped in the memories of a past unknown to anyone except the entity that lived there. Built on flat land near the banks of the Tombigbee, the house may have seen the likes of weary travelers as they made their way in riverboats past the small town of Fulton, Mississippi.

Perhaps the restless spirit was someone who had died there.   Stories of death and tragedy were not uncommon on the Tombigbee River and the ghosts of ill-fated souls were known legends.

Years spent living in the house produced plenty of unexplained paranormal activity.   The sound of footsteps on the stairs haunted the Bedford children each night as they lay awake waiting for the spirit to quieten.   Doors opening and closing could be heard all over the house, but no one was ever there.   And then the appearance of an unknown male who appeared in the home one day left the Bedford's unnerved as the young man asked to see one of the Bedford boys and called him by name, but no one had ever seen the mysterious young man and before anyone could ask his name, he disappeared.

Sometime later, the Bedford's moved to another home located on the North Road in Fulton, Mississippi and near the waterway marina.   The strange phenomena continued at the new home where the kids witnessed a rotary telephone dial on its own.

Each night the kids would awaken to the bedcovers pulled off of them and gathered in the floor.

Could an unseen spirit that was attached to this family be the cause of the Bedford hauntings? Ghosts are not limited to one location, but both of the houses that once entertained the presence of an unknown entity are no longer standing. The Bedford's say that the hauntings stopped years ago, and today they are happily ghost free.

The Haunting at Oakland Institute

Hidden behind the trees on Oakland School Road in Tremont, Mississippi is the former site of The Oakland Institute, a century old private institution. Established in 1887 by G.A. and J.T. Holley, the institute once provided a classical education in Art and Latin. The college also offered business and education courses that shaped the lives of many graduates who later became successful leaders across the southern United States. The original structure was a two-story building but was later torn down in 1930. Another one story structure took its place in the same location and served as a school educating children and youth to the eighth grade. In 1954, its doors finally closed forever.

For decades, stories have circulated around the eastern Itawamba county landmark. Its historic marker is located about a mile east of Tremont on Highway 23 North, but the site's ghostly phenomena has left an imprint that dozens have witnessed over the years.

The site is a popular hangout for kids and ghost hunters hoping to catch an apparition on camera. The old school is renowned for its creepiness and residual energy. Whispers and loud voices have been heard near a bathroom in the building, and some have said that the most haunted area of the building is the auditorium where ghostly figures have been seen. Doors have been known to slam shut upon entering the school, and the ghost of a little boy has been seen standing in a corner. Others have reported seeing the ghost of a man, but the most terrifying story known to exist involves a horrific and bloody scene that happened on an old road behind the Oakland Institute. According to the legend, a local pastor abused several children and then murdered them. The pastor was then lynched and hanged in a nearby tree. Could the ghostly man be the pastor still searching for more victims?

According to local folklore, the most prominent ghost of Oakland Institute is the spirit of a woman who walks the road in front of the institute every night. She carries a lantern in her hand and is often seen standing in front of the building when she suddenly vanishes. No one knows who the ghost lady may be, but members of the community have always said that she was probably one of the many teachers who taught at the distinguished school of higher learning.

The Haunting on Bowen Road

Brooke Adams had no way of knowing what was coming for her and her family when she moved into the small wood frame house once owned by her now deceased step-grandmother. Brooke and her family were only in the house for about four to five months, but the phenomena they experienced would never be forgotten.

Within weeks of moving in, paranormal activity spiked. A metal basket that Brooke used to store clothes hangers in randomly lifted up and slammed down against the floor. Other loud slamming noises echoed through the house and sounded as if someone was beating their fists against the bar in the kitchen. Brooke's dog, a Labrador retriever was also known to tuck its tail and run away from the kitchen area, and terror filled the house every night at approximately 10:00 p.m.

Each night that Brooke stepped into the bathroom shower to bathe, she heard the sound of someone running around the house and down the hall, but when she got out of the shower to investigate, she found her daughter sound asleep in her bed. There was no else in sight. Then at 10:00 p.m., violent crashing and slamming noises echoed from her daughter's bedroom as the baby bed slid back and forth against the wall.

One night when a family friend was sleeping over, she awakened to being choked by something or someone she could not see. She woke Brooke and vowed to never stay the night again if Brooke's husband was not home. Sometime later, Brooke's oldest daughter woke up crying and saying that she 'didn't want to see that man in black anymore'. Then Brooke's cousin encountered the entity when she was babysitting Brooke's youngest daughter one day.

While she was feeding the baby in the kitchen, the entity became exceptionally noisy as it pounded against the wall, bouncing from one spot to the next until it filled her cousin with a terror beyond anything she had experienced. She grabbed the baby and ran out of the house where she waited on the front porch until Brooke arrived home.

Weeks before she and her family abandoned the home, Brooke Adams hired a paranormal investigative team to explore the property. The team spent a few hours in the home setting up audio and video equipment. After the investigation was complete, the evidence was overwhelming as the team realized that they had caught the entity on video as it flipped one of their recording devices over. Audio equipment recorded the laughter and a direct response to one of the researcher's questions when he asked the spirit if it was the ghost of Brooke's late step-grandmother. The entity responded by saying 'yes' and then followed with menacing laughter.

Finally after weeks of hair-raising phenomena and Brooke awakening to the feeling of someone in the room with her, she and the family moved out. During her final moment in the house, Brooke Adams told the entity 'not to follow' her or her family to their new home. Although she and her family are free of the hauntings now, she believes the malevolent ghost still resides in the house on Bowen Road.

The Living Dead
at Ben Moore Road

For more than a century, the land surrounding Ben Moore Road has been home to settlers. The half mile road dead-ends now around a curve that leads to several homes. The small country neighborhood was developed in the 1980's by Pitts Realtors, but decades before, the area was used as farmland where soybeans, corn, and wheat grew with abundance.

In the mid-19th century, a large family built a dog trot cabin and lived in the area. Today, the only remaining sign of their existence is the family cemetery that houses the bones of three infants, a seven year-old girl, and the graves of other unidentified persons. While the graves are now grown over with lush green grass, the souls of those who once died here live on as restless spirits.

Numerous paranormal witnesses have experienced the hauntings in the old cabin. Situated across the road from more modern day houses, kids often played in the old house. An outhouse still stood in the back of the property with a box of newspapers that dated to the 1930's sitting just inside the door. A man's fedora hat and black coat hung on a wall inside the wellhouse, and the man's boots still sat in the corner as if he would be returning soon. But the sounds of footsteps may have indicated that he never left.

Nearby neighbors often shared stories of the man dressed in a black coat. He sometimes appeared in the front window of the cabin. Watching and waiting for something or somebody who never came. He terrorized ole' lady Madison, appearing behind her as she unloaded groceries from the trunk of her car. No one knew who he was or why his spirit appeared at random times, but he was always seen wearing the same Fedora hat and black coat that still hung on a rusted nail in the old wellhouse.

About five years later, a family of four bought the land that housed the cabin. Ed Parker, a local contractor and head of the household wasted no time as he made preparations to build their new house on the site. Within weeks, he cleared the land and demolished the old cabin. A concrete foundation was poured in its place.

Months later, the Parker's moved into their new brick home. Ed often sat on the outdoor patio and covered porch area facing the back of the property. Early one evening after supper, he was sitting alone on the back porch enjoying a beer and a vision of red and orange hues as the sunset painted the twilight sky. He rested in the rocking chair as he glided forward and backward while watching cattle graze in a nearby field. Then all of a sudden, a shadow caught his eye. He heard nothing, but he saw movement, and he jerked around to the left. His heart skipped a beat as he stared at the four foot tall apparition of a little girl dressed in a white flowing gown. She moved slow across the yard and did not seem to know that Ed Parker was present. He rubbed his eyes and closed them quickly, but she was still there now floating off the ground without visible feet.

Ed jumped out of this chair and ran inside the house. He slammed the door behind him and locked it. As his wife turned the corner of the kitchen and met him in the doorway, she stopped dead in her tracks at the sight of his pale face and apparent unease.

"What in the world is wrong, Ed? You look like you just saw a ghost!" Barbara noticed his hands shaking.

"I-I think I just did.   In the backyard."   Ed stuttered.

Barbara rushed to the window. Her eyes searched the yard from side to side. "I don't see anything."

"It was a girl. A little girl. I saw it." Ed rubbed his hands over his face.

Barbara huffed. "Well, I'll be. You must have scared her off."

That was the last time Ed Parker ever sat on the back porch alone.

Not long after Ed's encounter with the girl's ghost, other family members in the home began reporting doors opening and closing on their own. And the sound of footsteps was often heard in the hall at night. During a friend's overnight visit, the sound of an infant crying awakened her. She climbed out of bed and searched the house for the source of the noise but didn't find anything. Then as she entered the bedroom where she had been sleeping, something touched her and rubbed against the length of her back. She spent the rest of the night with her eyes wide open. When daylight came, she gathered her things and left. She never stayed overnight in the house again.

Today, the living dead of Ben Moore Road is believed to lay dormant. Just waiting to be awakened one more time.

THE END

Have you heard about this story?

The Haunting of Natalie Bradford was inspired by the 1974 real life murder of Liz Bradford and the haunting that turned Natalie Houston's life upside down. Natalie Houston wanted nothing more than a life of love and stability for herself and her children, but would life at Lindenwood be everything she had hoped for? Within days of moving in, the new Mrs. Bradford faces a treacherous, prophetic future and an introduction to the paranormal that she will never forget. Denial can be deadly.

FOREWORD

I began my research twenty-five years after Liz Bradford's death. Unknown to me, there was a hidden story within a story. The synchronistic findings were incredulous, and I found myself bewildered as I uncovered a prophecy that seemed to be predestined for Natalie Houston. Was she simply in the wrong place at the wrong time? Or, was she being used as an instrument to reveal a prophetic message?

My research carried me to the graveyard where Liz Bradford had been buried. I looked all around, not knowing which way to go. I closed my eyes and concentrated on the area while listening for my sixth sense to guide me. I then opened my eyes and walked directly to the site where Liz Bradford lay! A new tombstone was laid on Ms. Bradford's grave. It was larger than the old one I remembered, and it had an inscription.

Trees had grown to maturity from the hillside gravesite hiding the front view of an abandoned Lindenwood. The grass seemed to be greener and thicker than it was years ago, and I noticed a new bouquet of flowers resting at her headstone. I will never forget the uneasiness that swept over me as I stood in the same place where I had stood twenty-five years before.

Later, my research took me to the courthouse in search of the court records from Devon Bradford's trial. It took almost three weeks to locate the transcripts. Of all the files in the room, the Bradford case had mysteriously been misfiled in a box stacked out of place. I wondered if someone was trying to warn me to stay away. Each day I sat in the small, crowded storage room of the courthouse and studied the transcripts as if I was in a hypnotic trance. The more I read, the more scared I became. My research continued to turn up more and more bizarre coincidences that sent chills creeping up my back.

A few months after the first draft of this book was written, I came in contact with the bartender on duty the night Liz Bradford was murdered. During my interview with him, he told me that Liz Bradford's suitcase sat packed just inside his stepfather's office door. He said it sat there for many weeks, maybe even months. I was saddened for her. She never came back to pick it up.

Years later, I found myself living in a house behind The Rex Plaza where Liz Bradford was murdered. Not knowing the history of the house, my husband and I bought it as an investment and later found out it was haunted. I still do not know the origin of the spirit, but I can promise you, it scared the hell out of me. We lived there five years. Many days I sat on my redwood deck in the backyard of my home and gazed across the fence at the parking lot of the prestigious motel. I daydreamed of the days Liz Bradford once walked the floors of the lavishly decorated lounge serving cocktails to the wealthy guests and out of town patrons looking for some nightlife in Elvis's town.

I still visit the restaurant where she worked and try to imagine myself as a customer on the night she died.

The parking lot and facility is still standing in the same structure it was 38 years ago. The spirit of Liz Bradford is still prevalent to me when I walk in the restaurant.

Today, I live in a house that is ghost free. After many years of extensive study and dealing with the paranormal, I have to say I don't miss the unnerving chaos that ghosts can cause, but some ghosts such as the spirit of Liz Bradford need us to tell their stories. Sometimes, the person they pick to tell the story may not be a coincidence. Natalie Houston was a non-believer in the spiritual world, but she got an introduction that would change her thinking for the rest of her life and her sleep.

Sweet Dreams, Natalie.

CHAPTER 1

Liz Bradford wrestled against the stinging blows of her husband's hands. Tiny strands of dark brown hair lay scattered across the floor as Devon Bradford ripped them loose from her head. She cried out in pain.

"Stop!" She slapped at him only causing his fury to accelerate.

"If I can't have you, nobody will!" Devon shouted.

Liz moaned and forced herself out of the bedroom door. Devon picked up a nearby belt and began beating her with it. Swinging wildly as the leather snapped against her skin.

"Leave me alone! Stop!" She begged.

Devon stood over her staring at her with a loathing that promised deadly consequences if she left him. He wouldn't allow it. His mind was made up. He turned and walked away as Liz climbed onto the living room sofa.

She massaged the tender bruises and stinging pain on her face and head. She closed her eyes and vowed that she would escape tomorrow. She silently made her plans. When morning came, she would quickly get her things and drive to a friend's house in Tupelo. He wouldn't follow her there. If she could get away long enough, maybe she could figure out what she needed to do. Although her husband had accused her of seeing other men, she felt her marriage had been over for some time. People didn't know the man she knew.

Love had not been kind here, but would it be kind somewhere else? If she stayed, she might never know, but what would be the consequences of leaving? Liz began to drift to sleep. Hours seemed to pass like minutes. Liz awakened to find a calm silence within the house. The children were still sleeping as she hurriedly shoved piles of clothes into the truck. She had not seen Devon and wasn't about to concern herself with his whereabouts. It was time to leave before he returned.

She rushed up the stairs and walked to the side of her daughter's bed. Liz quickly sat down next to Susan gently shaking her awake.

Susan stirred. She rubbed her eyes and squinted at her mother. "What? What is it?"

Liz paused looking at her daughter. She felt an overwhelming sense of dread. "Honey, I just wanted to say Good-bye. This may be the last time that I see you."

Susan looked at her mother with disbelief. She leaned up and hugged her unaware of the reality in Liz's statement.

Liz Bradford turned and walked out the door. She was consumed with angst. Somehow she sensed that this day was the beginning of the end. Was it fear consuming her or the uncanny essence of premonition? She was unknowingly casting a spell of events beyond her control. It was now just a matter of hours before a prophecy would be born.

CHAPTER 2

Liz Bradford stepped onto the front lawn of her friend and co-worker, Rose Smith. She slammed the truck door shut. She had filled the front seat with clothes and a .25 mm handgun. Her feet seemed to skip as she neared the front door. Rose Smith was waiting for her on the front steps of her home.

"Oh, Liz. What has he done to you?" Rose reached for Liz's hand and beckoned for her to come inside.

"Nothing more than he usually does, but this time I've had enough. I mean it. I swear I'm not going back to him." Liz rubbed her fingers across the bruises that surrounded her neck and head. Bald patches covered various places about her head where Devon Bradford had pulled and stripped away her hair.

Rose shook her head in disbelief. She had heard that story before. How many times had she seen Liz Bradford shaken by a situation she didn't know how to escape from?

"All I've got to say is you're crazy if you do."

Rose looked tiny next to Liz's 5'7" frame. She led Liz to the living room where she invited her to sit down. She stopped in the kitchen and poured two cups of coffee before joining her.

Liz sighed. "You know, I've spent years with Devon, but I can't stand it anymore." Her eyes were misty as she put the hot coffee to her lips.

Liz cleared her throat. She wiped the corners of her eyes. Then just as quick, her expression changed into a vengeful stare. Her eyes focused on her friend, her lips pursed together. Her fingers curled tighter around the cup's handle. She thought about the night before when Devon had beat her head with his fists, his fury gaining momentum with each blow. He had left his humiliating tattoos on her for the last time.

"Rose, if you don't care, I want to stay here until I have to go to work this afternoon." Liz's eyes were glassy.

Rose nodded in agreement. "Of course you can."

"I said I wasn't going back. If he hurts me again, I swear I'll kill him."

Rose stared at her friend with unease. "I think you are in over your head, Liz. He may kill *you*. He's already told you he would."

Liz trembled. "I have a gun in the truck." She turned her eyes away and quickly looked back at Rose.

If he kills me, I'll come back for that bastard. I'll curse him for the rest of his life."

Rose felt a coldness sweep over her. Her stomach churned as she sat back in her chair. There was no more

doubting what might be coming. She now feared for Liz's life.

Meanwhile, Devon Bradford contemplated the day's events. His wife had packed her clothes and left, but she would be back. He was sure of it. If she refused, he would surely kill her. She would not humiliate him or disrespect him by leaving. Especially for another man.

He lifted the hood on the pale blue Chevy Impala. He busied himself with routine maintenance and repairs on the family's vehicle. Devon had a way of seeming taller than he actually was. At near 6'0, he exuded a presence unlike other men. He was a master of disguise leaving some women enchanted by his charisma and striking good looks. Devon stood back and stretched. The white cotton shirt often referred to as a 'wifebeater' that he frequently wore was soiled with oil and grime. He tossed the cigarette butt he had been gripping in his teeth to the ground. It was getting late. Liz would be going to work and he would be joining her just before midnight. In less than six hours, the stage would be set and the drama would include a whole new cast of characters in her story.

CHAPTER 3

December 21st, 1974, approximately 11:30 p.m.

Liz Bradford swung her hands in the air as the stinging blows swept across her face. She cried out with each blow, her head and neck still tender from the night before. Her butler style uniform of black and white satin was wrinkled and soiled with splotches of blood that dripped from her nose. She was fighting a battle she was sure to lose, but she was determined to leave Devon Bradford and his controlling ways. She had made up her mind, and nothing he could say or do was going to stop her.

The parking lot of the glamorous Rex Plaza was almost empty. Only the streetlights glowed in the foreground of the white brick motel, and the nautical style brass lanterns hanging outside the front door cast a soft light on the lot. The motel's guests were quiet in their rooms with few lights still shining through the curtains. The faint sound of Elvis Presley's *Jailhouse Rock* could be heard just outside the front door to the lounge known as The Lion's Den. No one inside the motel could hear Liz's screams, and there was no one outside to stop Devon Bradford.

Liz dropped her cigarette. Her hair was being ripped from her head. She kept swinging her long slender arms and hands in front of her face desperately trying to block the blows, but she wasn't strong enough. She felt his hands tightening around her neck. Her mind raced as the breath was being choked from her lungs. She struggled with a force greater than she ever had before. He couldn't get away with this any longer. How many times had she narrowly escaped strangulation? She gasped for air and felt the heat rise in her face as her chestnut eyes began to water. Still slinging her arms about, she swept her hands across the seat beside her to find the .25 caliber pistol she had been carrying. She swung it around, but Devon was too quick. His hands were on the barrel pulling the gun from her grip. Liz screamed out. She twisted her body quickly as she got on her knees and began to climb in the backseat of the Chevy Impala. If she didn't escape fast, he would kill her. Her feet scraped the dashboard of the car as she maneuvered herself over the seat. Time seemed to stand still as fear paralyzed her movements. She felt herself moving in slow motion. She whimpered, mouthing words to herself.

"No, No. This can't-"

"Bitch!" Devon Bradford's icy blue eyes were filled with rage, his mouth clenched as he struck her.

Hate and jealously fueled his fury as he gripped the 25 mm pistol. He wouldn't let her get away with the humiliation she had caused him. She would not make a fool out of him in his own hometown. The thought of his wife being with another man was too much for his ego. He had an image he had to uphold. Everyone in the community knew Devon Bradford. He was the reason all of Liz's friends envied her.

Liz screamed. She heard only one shot. Fleeting memories passed through her mind like a movie reel. Her eyes began to close as she screamed in silence one last time in an effort to awaken from a nightmare that would not end. Her body suddenly became limp from the sharp stabbing pains in her back. Saliva began to ooze out of her mouth as tears spilled from her eyes and mucus dripped from her long slender nose. Streaks of mascara ran down her face that had been carefully painted with dark, pink rouge and red lipstick for her night's work as a waitress at the classiest restaurant in town. Her head lay over the front seat facing the back windshield. Another shot rang out. With the second shot, Liz Bradford was dead.

"Central to Baker Three." The urgency in the dispatcher's voice alerted Officer Roy Wilson. Although the streets had been clearing for a couple of hours, it was still a weekend that meant an increase in the number of calls for the police. With Christmas just four days away, city streets had kept the department busier than usual.

"Baker Three, go ahead, Central."

"Respond to The Rex Plaza, 619 North Gloster. A subject was found in the parking lot. Condition is unknown. Emergency crew is in route."

"10-4, Central. I'm on my way." Wilson wiped sweat from his forehead. Being a large man with arthritis in his knees and a hot-nature that only an Alaskan vacation could soothe, it wasn't uncommon to see the officer wiping his forehead from time to time even in the dead of winter.

Wilson slammed his foot against the gas pedal. The tires of his 1973 Chevy Impala screeched as he sped down the highway. Sirens from other patrol cars echoed through the city streets as fellow officers assisted Wilson to the scene. He flew into the parking lot, flinging his car door open and hurriedly walked over to the area where a few bystanders stood watching. The temperature outside was only 33 degrees, but Wilson was pulling his jacket off. The cold air created a fog each time he breathed out of his mouth.

Wilson stood over Devon Bradford. The wounded man was lying face down on the pavement. He nudged him with his foot. Devon could only moan. He was drifting in and out of consciousness. Wilson kneeled beside his body and rolled him over. He looked over Devon and touched his chest. His brown flannel shirt was saturated with blood.

"This man's been shot! Wilson shouted to the other officers who had already arrived and were approaching the scene. Where's that damn ambulance?"

Wilson grabbed his radio. "Central, have you notified the detective division?

"10-4, Baker Three, David 3 is on call. He's on his way."

"10-4. A man has been shot." Wilson was loud, speaking fast and breathless into the microphone.

Seconds later, the flashing red lights from the ambulance could be seen from a short distance along with Detective Bobby Johnson trailing behind in his unmarked patrol unit. Johnson sped into the parking lot. He left his car door open and headed to Wilson's side. His long gray hair was tightly wrapped in a ponytail with a leather shoestring. Dressed in denim and a jacket with a dream catcher emblem on the back, he was known as the renegade in the department. His love for the Native American Indian was exemplified in his appearance. Johnson puffed on his cigarette as he looked around at the crowd that was gathering. By now, a few guests and employees had gathered in the front parking lot of the motel.

Officer Wilson stepped back from the man's body as paramedics pushed past the officers. He towered over the scene, looking like a linebacker for the Dallas Cowboys as he stood nearby watching while the paramedics began to check Devon's motionless body for a pulse.

"We've got a weak pulse on this guy," the paramedic shouted. He noticed the gunshot wounds and began to cut Devon's shirt from his body. His shirt and undershirt were clearly soaked with blood. The bullet holes in the material were precise.

"I'll take that shirt." Johnson stepped forward as the paramedic flung the shirt away from the wounded man's body. He glanced at the detective with irritation.

The emergency crew continued to work frantically to get Devon Bradford on the stretcher. As he watched the paramedics load the man in the ambulance, Johnson overheard one of them say the man had been shot in the chest. Then without warning, a shout came from across the parking lot.

"Liz! Liz has been shot!"

Wilson jerked around to see where the commotion was coming from. His knees cracked and throbbed as he ran to the blue Chevy Impala. He jerked on the driver's side door, but the door was jammed. A huge dent was in the front fender of the driver's side. He went around to the passenger side and shined a flashlight into the car. The still body of a woman hanging over the front seat stunned the officer. A pistol lay on the seat just inches away from her body.

"I need some help over here! We need another ambulance!" Wilson yelled, wiping his forehead. He laid his flashlight on the ground and reached in the car for Liz's arm.

A paramedic ran over to help Wilson pull the body from the car. He immediately noticed the gunshot wounds and placed his fingers on Liz's neck to check for a pulse while fumbling to get his stethoscope on her chest. The gunshot wound to the head had inflicted a perfect round hole behind her left ear.

There was no pulse. Her eyes were slightly open. He carefully placed his fingers on her eyelids and pulled her lids fully open to inspect her pupils. Her eyes had already been set. Her skin appeared pale with traces of blue. He cleared his voice. "She's dead. Probably been dead a good thirty minutes or so."

The paramedic shook his head and backed away. "I'll radio the hospital to send another ambulance." His tone was regretful as he thought of the approaching holidays.

Wilson stood still with his hands on his holster belt while Captain Ray Sullivan who had just arrived moments earlier puffed on his cigarette. He stood at a distance and quietly supervised the scene. He was a quiet man and highly respected by his subordinates. He treated the younger officers like they were his children rather than his employees, always watching out for them and even hosting frequent cookouts for everyone on the shift. He was 6' 3" tall with a strong manly presence and charismatic air. It wasn't uncommon for women to show their appreciation for his rugged good looks. Women flirted incessantly with him.

Sullivan's deep-set dark eyes were fixed on the body of Liz Bradford. He studied the scene for a moment and pondered over the position of Devon Bradford's body and how Liz Bradford had just been discovered. He ran his fingers across his lips, and there was no doubt that he was forming an opinion of what had just happened at The Rex Plaza.

Sullivan flicked his cigarette to the ground and started for the door to the lounge. The heavy wooden door slowly eased shut as he stepped inside the front foyer. The motel housekeepers were busy dusting the ornate frames of the oil paintings hanging in the foyer and cleaning the tile floor. Trickles of water could be heard from the built-in wall fountain beside the hostess's desk. A faint scent of sweet cigars lingered in the air from the dining room. Majestic, ornate buffets and various antique pieces made of cherry wood filled the restaurant. Each piece was hand carved to perfection. Italian style chairs were pushed carefully under the round tables covered with crisp, white linen tablecloths. Inside the dining hall, the hard wood floors were being polished. The windows were covered with folds of rich, burgundy colored velvet trimmed in fringe and tassels. It was a setting for the elite and the romantic at heart.

The last two waitresses in the restaurant were busy setting the tables with spotless goblets and wine stems. Sullivan looked over his head. The brass and glass chandeliers provided just the right amount of light for a romantic experience the motel was famous for. The motel was voted as the "most romantic dining experience in town". It wasn't any wonder that Sullivan had been here several times for domestic disputes. Husbands had come through the back door of the lounge many times only to be met by their wives waiting in the hall. Love and war was famous at The Rex Plaza. It was Tupelo's hot spot, a town of slightly more than 20,000 people where most people knew each other. There was a lot of old money in Tupelo. A person with any clout at all was often courted at The Rex Plaza and showered with attention. And for those married 'wanna be bachelors' that didn't want the trouble that the front door entrance could cause, The Rex Plaza provided a back door entrance/exit.

Elvis Presley had put Tupelo on the map having been born on the East side in a shack. He often spoke fondly of his hometown when he recounted his boyhood days at Shake Rag where the black community welcomed the future King of Rock –n- Roll. He had frequented The Rex Plaza along with Johnny Cash and others who wanted to play some late night poker in Room 105. Although Elvis was not seen in Tupelo very often, his portraits were proudly displayed in the motel's foyer.

Sullivan walked toward the door to the bar and gently eased the door open as it creaked inch by inch. The bartender glanced up at Sullivan as he twisted a rag in a wine glass polishing it to perfection for the next guest. He reached above his head and placed the glass stem in the overhang. The bar was quite large for the small room, the dance floor only wide enough to accommodate about twenty people.

The bartender adjusted the eyeglasses that sat firmly against his nose. His black bow tie hung to the side of his collar. The front of his white shirt still looked freshly pressed except for the sleeves twisted half-way up his arms.

"May I help you?" Ben Johnson's voice was more hoarse than usual. His voice was unforgettable with its soft, raspy tone, and his typical way of looking at someone from a sideways glance made him almost resemble a snapshot from Hollywood's lost archive.

He pushed the sleeves further up his arms as he reached to empty dirty ashtrays lined across the bar top. He wasn't surprised to see the officer and had wondered if they would come in the lounge to talk to anyone about the incident.

"Yeah, I hope so. Sullivan walked over to the bar and pulled up a barstool. I need to ask you a couple of questions. Maybe you can help me out."

Ben shrugged his shoulders. "Sure."

"The waitress out front—did you know her?"

"Liz? Yes, sir, she worked here." Ben cleared his throat.

"Did you know her husband?"

"No. I recognized him when he came in the restaurant from time to time. He was an odd fellow. Kinda sneaky acting and mean." Ben continued to polish the top of the bar then stopped and looked Sullivan dead in the face.

Sullivan stared back. "How so?"

Ben propped his hands on the counter and looked at the ceiling studying the tiles of pressed tin. "Liz told us about him beating her. She mentioned that he was real jealous. He came in tonight looking for her." Ben paused and studied Sullivan.

"Did you talk to him?"

"Yeah, he just asked me if I knew where she was, and I told him no. You know, she always seemed scared of him." Ben shook his head with sympathy for Liz.

Sullivan wrote in a small spiral notebook. "What did he do then?"

"He just turned around and left. I didn't see him again. Then, my step dad came running in an hour later saying that a man was lying in the parking lot." Ben pointed toward the door. He shook his head again with remorse. "I sure do hate this happened. Poor Liz. She was a sweet lady. Never gave us a minute's trouble."

"How long had she worked here?"

"Just a few months."

Sullivan flipped the notebook shut. "Thanks. If you think of anything else, here's my card." He turned and walked out the door. He adjusted his gun holster as he stood staring down the well-lit city street. His next stop must be North Mississippi Medical Center, the city's only hospital and the region's closest major medical center.

CHAPTER 4

It was approximately 1:15 a.m., and Devon Bradford lay quiet as Natalie Houston pushed the stretcher down the long corridor. His moaning and grunting had ceased as he fell into a light sleep. She glanced down at her patient and allowed her eyes to roam the length of his body. She noticed his nose, a bit large for his face. He reminded her of an Indian man she once knew, tall and dark with a distinguished nose. His thick hair was coal black with traces of gray, and his shirt had been cut off him to reveal a stunning manly chest, thick with hair the same color as his head. His olive toned skin was smooth and dark as if he had just spent a few hours in the sunshine. Natalie took a deep breath as she admired all she had been noticing. Dark men had always been her weakness, even the ones not worth getting to know.

The doors to the operating room swung open. "What we got here, girls?" Dr. Jay Adams asked as he hurriedly walked around the gurney. The thoracic surgeon had already been in the hospital when the ambulance arrived. He was a short, stocky man with graying hair and a cocky, aristocratic attitude. He thought most people weren't as smart as he was. He was known about the hospital for being volatile and untrustworthy as a friend. And if he didn't like someone as a co-worker, they had better be prepared for the sabotage he could create in their career. But, if there was anything worth respecting about Dr. Jay Adams, it was his dedication to his job and his determination to save lives. He and Natalie had that in common.

"He's been shot in the chest, Dr. Adams. I was downstairs when they brought him in." Natalie watched as the doctor bent over the quiet body of Devon Bradford.

Dr. Adams lightly touched the area surrounding the three bullet holes. The wounds were small, but precise. He placed the strips of gauze back in place until the techs got ready to shave his chest.

Dr. Adams grumbled under his breath. "Looks like this is going to take a few hours." He turned and looked at Natalie who stood near the corner of the room with her hands clasped together. She looked toward the floor while waiting for his instruction.

"How much coffee you had, Ms. Houston?"

"Enough", she said frowning. "Enough. In fact, I was on my coffee break when they brought him in." She ran her fingers over her surgery cap in search of a free strand of her shoulder length brown hair. She felt uneasy around Dr. Adams and tried to avoid him as much as she could. She had heard about his reputation and didn't care to be his next victim.

"You know what happened to this guy?" Dr. Adams began to scrub his hands.

"I was told he was shot at The Rex Plaza."

Dr. Adams laughed to himself. He looked up and mockingly replied. "Well, I'd say you're certainly on top of things, Nurse Houston. It's obvious he was shot. What else can you tell us?"

Natalie's face turned red. She wanted to tell him to go to hell, but he was the doctor, the boss, and some battles weren't worth fighting when it came to risking her job.

She hesitated. "I- I really don't know anything else. Sorry."

Dr. Adams ignored her and walked around the table. Natalie followed, getting into position for surgery. Even after years as a nurse, she still couldn't get over the initial shock of the knife in the operating room. The thought of her patient dying bothered her. On several occasions, she had left the hospital only to have dreams of her patients. She never considered that the dead were trying to thank her. She didn't believe in ghosts. If there was a spiritual world, the souls of the deceased had to be either in heaven or hell. There couldn't be any other place. At least, that's what she had been taught in the small Southern Baptist churches she had always attended. Her brother was a Baptist minister, and if he didn't know the Truth, no one did.

Five hours passed. Natalie Houston stood over Devon Bradford. She focused her eyes on her patient and watched as Dr. Adams removed the three bullets from Devon Bradford's chest. With an unmatched skill, Dr. Adams removed the last bullet and dropped it in the metal tray that Natalie held. The metal reacted like a bell ringing as each bullet had dropped against the flat, stainless steel plate. The clinking seemed loud in the room almost creating an echo. Minutes seemed to pass like hours as Dr. Adams closed Devon's chest. The surgery had been a success. Devon's wounds had not been critical. His vital signs were satisfactory, but he had lost a lot of blood. He would have to be transferred to intensive care for at least 24 hours.

Natalie took a deep breath. Her eyes had become heavy, and her feet were aching. She smiled to herself. She had assisted in saving another life. It felt good. She paused to study her patient and wondered what had led to his being shot. She wondered who he was. Not his name, but who was the man asleep on the table in front of her? Had he been a victim? She quickly brushed off her thoughts. There had been many times she had wondered things about her patients, but it wasn't her business to know her patient's personal affairs. Her responsibility was saving lives.

Dr. Adams sighed heavily and began to yank off his gloves as he made his way to the door. Natalie felt her shoulders relax as she followed behind the doctor. Her upper back ached from being bent over the operating table. She still suffered her own agony with a slipped disc from a couple of years ago. Her back had never been the same since the injury. She was tired and fatigued that day, and she didn't realize the weight of the old man she was bathing when she pulled him from the tub. It happened quickly, and it cost her six weeks off work recuperating from back surgery.

Natalie stretched her hands over her head. She pulled off her surgical gloves and turned on the hot water in the large stainless steel sink. She scrubbed her hands vigorously as her mind drifted back to the patient on the table. A mixture of emotions suddenly swept over her. Grief. Confusion. Attraction. She was bewildered. It was as if she was being manipulated by something outside herself. Feeling things that were not her own. Natalie let out a sigh. She summed up the strange new awareness to long hours and tired feet. A long hot bath would do her well. And sleep. Yes, she needed sleep.

But, she should have listened to what she couldn't hear. She should have been aware of that heightened thing called instinct. Instead, she was blindfolded by her own incognizance. She was walking steadfast into a treacherous future being revealed before her very eyes.

CHAPTER 5

It was early Christmas Eve morning. While Devon Bradford lay quiet in his hospital room bed, the family and friends of Liz Bradford gathered at the church just down the highway from the mansion that once belonged to Liz Bradford. Lindenwood had been hers, built with the children in mind. It was her dream home, and all she had ever wanted other than a love she had not found. The Bradford children reluctantly prepared for their mother's funeral. James Bradford put on his finest shirt and tie not sure that it matched. The eighteen-year old son had the sole responsibility of getting his three other sisters to the funeral on time. Rebecca finished brushing her hair and left her room to check on Susan and Audrey, her two younger sisters. They were all just three years apart with Rebecca recently turning fourteen. As the sisters walked to the front door of the house, the door swung open with a gust of wind. The girls jumped. A force of wind swept across their faces, bitter cold and dry. Rebecca rushed to shut the door. A mournful howling could be heard as the wind swept through the upstairs of the mansion across the banister and out the upstairs balcony.

"What was that?" Rebecca yelled across the room. Audrey and Susan shrugged their shoulders and pulled their jackets tighter across their chests.

Rebecca shivered. "We better get going. James is probably waiting for us outside." The wind's howl had unnerved her with its distinct cry.

Rebecca slammed the door behind them. They crossed the front yard and got into James's 1965 Mustang. "What took you so long?" His voice was agitated.

"Nothing. Just drive." Rebecca shot back.

The drive was short, across the highway and up the hill. The small church held the body of Liz Bradford and the several family members and friends that had gathered to say goodbye. Liz's grave had been dug the day before. Her body was to be buried beside her deceased daughter, Caroline Bradford. The fourteen-year-old girl had drowned the year before.

As James parked the Mustang, Audrey sat staring out the window at the graveyard across from the church. Her face reflected a somber frown in the pane of glass, her dark brown hair and eyes a living reflection of their mother's features.

She chewed on her finger as she studied the mound of dirt that had been poured for her mother's grave. Her sister's grave still had bare spots where the grass had not grown back. She remembered the familiar green tent that stood over the gravesite. The graves were at the far side of the graveyard and could be seen from the upstairs bay window at Lindenwood. Tears of longing and grief swept over Audrey.

"Audrey, let's go." Rebecca nudged Audrey in the arm. Audrey opened the door of the car and slid off the seat. Her grandmother was waiting for her on the front steps of the church.

Moments later, the Bradford children escorted by Liz's mother entered the church where their mother lay resting among mounds of funeral wreaths. The fresh flowers emitted a strong sweet odor throughout the parlor and brightened the softly lit scene with blues, pinks, and blues. A few red and ivory poinsettias were placed near the casket casting a dreadful memory of Christmas for the children. Mourners lined the hallway waiting to pay their last respects to the deceased mother of six children, a daughter and wife, and a hairdresser for many in the community who came to see Liz when she wasn't working at The Rex Plaza.

The soft murmurs of people's chatter filled the church parlor. There was an eerie unease in the air as several visitors whispered. Questions filled the minds of those closest to Liz and Devon Bradford. Had Devon killed her? Did he catch her with another man? Was there any way that Liz could have realistically left her husband without suffering this type of demise? Everyone seemed to have their own opinions about what had happened. The rumors were already circulating around the community. Some believed that Devon had killed Liz and then shot himself. Others believed that someone else had shot Devon Bradford after he killed Liz.

Everyone had a theory, but the people who knew the truth were either not talking or dead. Audrey made her way to the casket. Her face mirrored the horror and grief of a newly orphaned child. Thoughts raced through her mind. Tomorrow was Christmas. It would not be worth remembering but would become a part of her for the remainder of her life. She stood quiet with her hands clasped. Tears flooded her eyes. Her mother was gone, and her dad was now absent resting in a hospital bed while she and four other children watched as their mother was lowered into the earth. What would happen to her without her mother? Audrey studied her mother. The reality of death frightened her. She wondered how scared her mom must have been when she died.

Liz's body had been carefully prepared. Her make-up was heavy with her lips having been painted a crimson red, but the dark rouge Liz Bradford always wore was absent this morning. Her hair was combed neat and sprayed stiff with hairspray against her head, unlike the way Liz fixed it herself in her own shop at Lindenwood. The children had selected a light blue dress to cover her tall full frame. Although her thick dark hair had been styled to cover the bullet wound, the perfect round hole behind her left ear had inflicted an exit wound on the opposite side of the temple. The burns and bruises on her skin could still be easily detected. As Audrey examined her mother's lifeless figure, she reached out to touch her mother's hand. It wasn't the same hand she remembered. Her hands were cold now and hard. And her mouth had been sewn shut in a dull, expressionless manner. Liz Bradford's lips were silent, but little did anyone know the quiet Liz Bradford would soon be making a grand entrance right back in the Lindenwood mansion where she belonged.

Get links to the rest of this story at LSydneyFisher.com

Have you heard about this story?

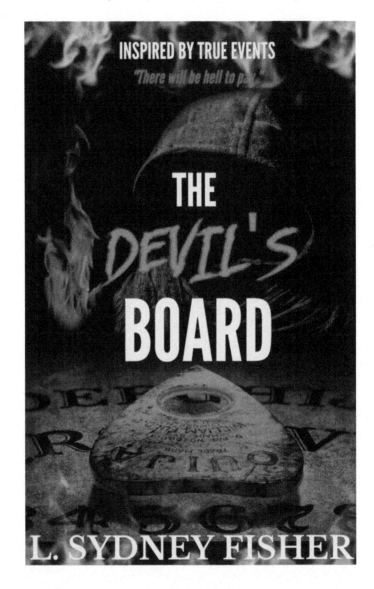

Don't miss this story that has people talking on college campuses everywhere! NOW a #1 Bestseller in Supernaturalism.

Experience the terror of *The Devil's Board* in this new supernatural thriller from the Amazon #1 Bestselling Author, L. Sydney Fisher.

Inspired by TRUE EVENTS.
On an American college campus in 1987, three students began playing a seemingly innocent game of contacting the dead. Word spread fast around campus and curiosity grew, expanding the group to more than forty people. Spirits were summoned almost daily, and the dark world's influence began to take its toll as one student fell gravely ill and relationships began to crumble. Months later, the dead would be resurrected, and this time there would be Hell to pay.

This is their story.

Note from Sydney~*The Devil's Board* is based on true events that happened in the Fall/Spring year of 1987-88. The college campus is located in small town, USA. To this day, the story of Ryan Banks still remains a haunting mystery. All names and locations have been changed to protect the privacy of the institution and the characters of the story. Some parts of *The Devil's Board* have been dramatized for the sake of storytelling.

SLEEP WITH THE LIGHTS ON!

Have you heard about this story?

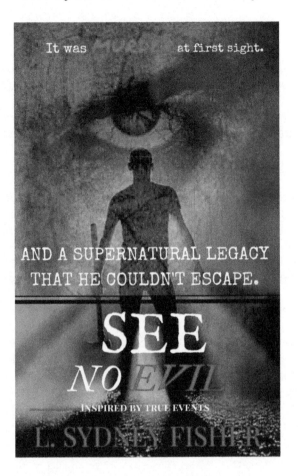

A story inspired by the real life Mississippi Mystic, Seymour Prater. Known throughout the South for his mysterious and miraculous abilities, he could "see" beyond the barriers of time and space while identifying a man's killer, finding stolen objects, and even locating lost people. Seymour Prater left behind a supernatural legacy and one unsolved murder that terrified a Mississippi town as the community battled their fears of the living and a dead man's ghost that haunted the 'Old Floyd Place'.

ABOUT THE AUTHOR

My ghost story began over twenty years ago.

"I first witnessed the paranormal at the tender age of eight. This experience unlocked a doorway to a world full of unexplained mysteries, miraculous insights, and terrifying ghostly visits that have spanned a lifetime. Join me as I explore these stories...one book at a time." ~L. Sydney Fisher

L Sydney Fisher is the #1 bestselling author of *The Haunting of Natalie Bradford.* Her love affair with reading and writing began at an early age. This insatiable desire for knowledge launched a curiosity into the world of the supernatural and unexplained that has spanned a lifetime. Sydney has a B.A. in English from The University of Mississippi and a Master's in Education from The University of Missouri.

Sydney lives on a haunted landscape with the spirit of a white wolf and at least one ghost that shares what was once a Native American village in Northeast, Mississippi. When she isn't writing, she's researching supernatural mysteries or another haunted location and its history.

Made in the USA
Las Vegas, NV
06 February 2021